Contents

How to use this book

Each page has a title telling you what it is about.

Instructions look like this. Always read these carefully before starting.

Read these word problems very carefully. Decide how you will work out the answers.

This shows you how to set out your work. The first question is done for you.

Ask your teacher if you need to do these.

This shows that the activity is an **Explore**. Work with a friend.

Sometimes there is a **Hint** to help you.

This means you must decide how to lay out your work and show your workings.

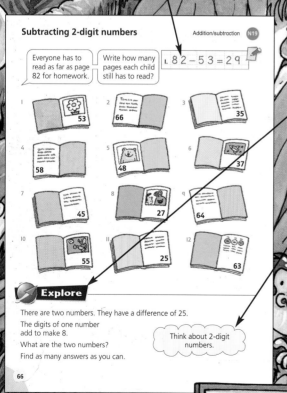

Sometimes you need materials to help you.

Place-value cards

4-digit numbers

Write how many thousands, hundreds, tens and units.

Place-value cards

£3681

1. £3000
   £ 600
   £ 80
   £   1

2. £6699
3. £1279
4. £1855
5. £4537

6. £4507
7. £2016
8. £7110
9. £3805

Write the numbers in order, from smallest to largest.

£1279, £1855, ...

Write the number made with each set of cards.

10. 2000 4 700 60

10. 2764

11. 4000 200 9 20
12. 3 90 900 5000
13. 40 4 8000 600
14. 100 7 10 1000

15. 2 5000 80
16. 7000 60 900
17. 6 1000 400
18. 4000 700 20

Write the numbers in order, from smallest to largest.

1117, 1406, ...

𝓮 Write all the numbers on the page in order.

3

4-digit numbers

Write the value of the <u>red</u> digit on each train.

1. | 7 | 0 | 0 |

1 **4768**

2 **8561**

3 **3972**

4 **4013**

5 **6690**

6 **9999**

7 **2803**

8 **3772**

9 **6960**

10 **7241**

Write the train numbers in order, from smallest to largest.

ℓ Write a number **between** each of the ordered numbers.

Explore

Use the cards shown to make all the possible numbers:

11 between 2000 and 2500

12 between 2500 and 3000

13 between 3000 and 3500

14 beyond 3500.

3000   100

2000   700

3   5   60   90

4-digit numbers

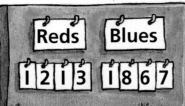 Write '<' or '>' between each pair.

1. 1 2 1 3 < 1 8 6 7

Reds **1213** Blues **1867**

Remember, Crocodile faces the **largest** number.

5 10

2  Reds **1975** Blues **1933**

3 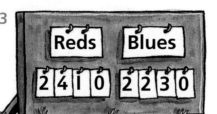 Reds **2410** Blues **2230**

4  Reds **3014** Blues **3118**

5 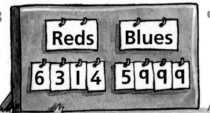 Reds **3667** Blues **3676**

6  Reds **4110** Blues **4100**

7 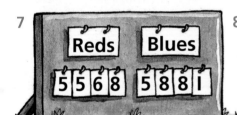 Reds **5568** Blues **5881**

8  Reds **6314** Blues **5999**

9 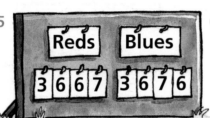 Reds **8006** Blues **8600**

🖉 Who won on each scoreboard, and by how many points?

Write each pair and write a possible missing digit.

10 38 0 > 3880

10. 3 8 9 0 > 3 8 8 0

11 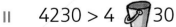 4230 > 4 30

12 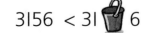 3156 < 31  6

13 2899 < 29 3

14  3052 > 3 2

15 4548 < 4  4

16 83 9 < 835

4-digit numbers

Write each number in figures.

1 Four thousand, three hundred and ninety-two

1. 4 3 9 2

2 One thousand, five hundred and eighty-four

3 Five thousand, one hundred and thirty-six

4 Eight thousand, seven hundred and forty-four

5 Nine thousand, two hundred and twenty

6 Three thousand, five hundred

7 Two thousand, eight hundred and ninety

8 Six thousand and thirty

Write the numbers in order, from smallest to largest.

?

Write each number in words.

9

5 2 7 1
miles

9. Five thousand, two hundred and seventy-one miles

10 8 3 4 3 miles

11 2 5 7 0 miles

12 6 6 9 4 miles

13 5 1 4 0 miles

14 2 6 0 3 miles

15 3 3 1 7 miles

● Each car travels 10 more miles. Write the new readings.

Adding to I0

Copy and complete.

1 8 + = I0

I. $8 + 2 = I0$

2   + 6 = I0

3   + I = I0

4 3 + = I0

5 + I0 = I0

6 4 + = I0

7 5 + = I0

8 7 + = I0

9 + 9 = I0

I0 2 + = I0

Write how much more to make 20p.

II  8p

II. $8p + I2p = 20p$

I2  5p

I3  4p

I4  Ip

I5  7p

I6  2p

I7  6p

Explore

0 1 2 3 4 5 6 7 8 9

Use any of the cards shown.
Write different ways to make 20 by adding.

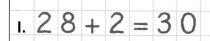

Comics are put in the van in multiples of 10.

Write how many must be added to each pile.

I. $28 + 2 = 30$

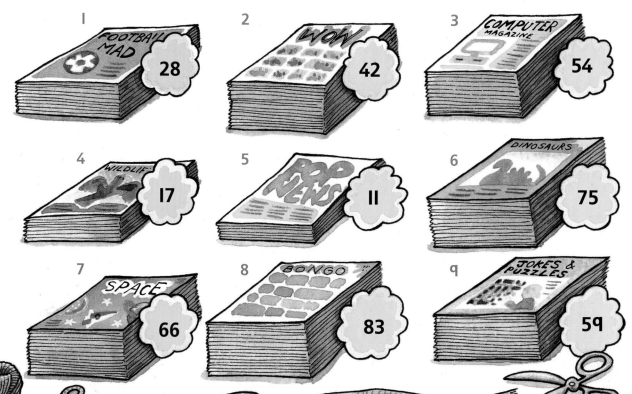

1 28

2 42

3 54

4 17

5 11

6 75

7 66

8 83

9 59

Copy and complete.

10 $43 + \boxed{} = 50$

10. $43 + 7 = 50$

11 $66 + \boxed{} = 70$

12 $\boxed{} + 15 = 20$

13 $38 + \boxed{} = 40$

14 $\boxed{} + 92 = 100$

15 $54 + \boxed{} = 60$

16 $\boxed{} + 27 = 30$

17 $\boxed{} + 75 = 80$

18 $61 + \boxed{} = 70$

19 $41 + \boxed{} = 50$

Adding to the next ten

The cash machine only gives multiples of 10.

Each person needs the amount shown.

They will get more than they need. Write how much more.

1. £24 + £6 = £30,   £6 more

1. £24
2. £42
3. £58
4. £17
5. £73
6. £36
7. £45
8. £63
9. £94
10. £88
11. £29
12. £51

Problems

13. Jane has **63p**.

She needs **70p** to buy a comic.

How much must she borrow?

14. Timo has **74p**.

He spends **12p** on a badge.

Then he wants to buy some football stickers. They cost **70p**.

How much more must he save?

15. Matthew makes a tape.

He uses up **73** minutes.

The final song finishes the tape. The tape is **80 minutes** long.

How long was the song?

Finding the difference

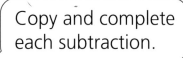

Copy and complete each subtraction.

I. $135 - 128 = 7$

1

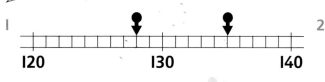

120   130   140

$135 - 128 =$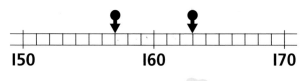

2

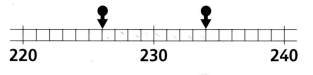

220   230   240

$234 - 226 =$

3

180   190   170

$181 - 173 =$

4

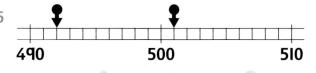

150   160   170

$163 - 157 =$

5

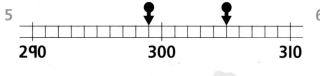

290   300   310

$305 - 299 =$

6

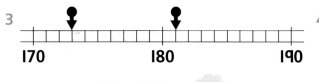

490   500   510

$- = $

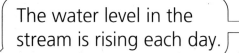

The water level in the stream is rising each day.

Write the difference in level between the days.

Monday
76 cm

Tuesday
92 cm

Wednesday
104 cm

?

Thursday
110 cm

Friday
111 cm

Saturday
122 cm

Sunday
134 cm

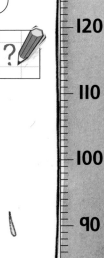

130

120

110

100

90

80

Finding the difference

> Write the difference between each set of scores.

1. $226 - 217 = 9$

1

Player 1	Player 2
226	217

2
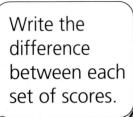

Player 1	Player 2
178	184

3

Player 1	Player 2
232	226

4

Player 1	Player 2
151	144

5

Player 1	Player 2
247	253

6

Player 1	Player 2
333	326

7

Player 1	Player 2
116	125

🄮 Write some pairs of scores with a difference of 4 points.

> Each child tries to win a prize.

> Write how many more points they need to reach the next prize.

Shahid 122

Tim 133

Yasmin 141

Jane 136

Jobe 142

Mel 146

150

145

140

135

130

125

Finding the difference

Each child has a set of raffle tickets to sell.

They have all sold their first ticket. Write how many more they must sell.

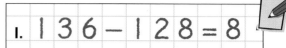

I. $136 - 128 = 8$

1. 128 — 136

2. 215 — 223

3. 237 — 243

4. 348 — 355

5. 188 — 192

6. 266 — 273

7. 376 — 383

8. 447 — 452

9. 325 — 333

Problems

10. I started with 123 stickers. I bought 8 more. Then 125 blew away! How many do I have left?

11. I had 240 stickers. I gave 224 to Matty. How many do I have now?

12

Adding pairs to 100 and 1000

Copy and complete each table. Continue the pairs until you reach the last one.

Table 1

Pairs to 100

$0 + 100 = 100$

$5 + 95 = 100$

$10 + 90 = 100$

$15 + = 100$

$20 + = 100$

$25 + = 100$

$95 + = 100$

$100 + = 100$

Table 2

Pairs to 1000

$0 + 1000 = 1000$

$50 + 950 = 1000$

$100 + 900 = 1000$

$150 + = 1000$

$200 + = 1000$

$250 + = 1000$

$950 + = 1000$

$1000 + = 1000$

e Write what you notice.

Write the matching pair to make 100.

a

45

a. 45, 55

b

95

c

40

d

35

e

75

f

15

g

20

h

10

i

65

j

85

k

70

l

55

Each elephant wants I litre of water to drink.

Write how much more each elephant needs.

I litre = 1000 ml

1. $350 + 650 = 1000$ ml

1. 350 ml
2. 250 ml
3. 150 ml
4. 550 ml
5. 400 ml
6. 650 ml
7. 200 ml
8. 450 ml

Gran wanted all the children to have £100 in total. Write how much she gave each.

9. £85

9. MONEY £15 BOX
10. £55
11. £36
12. £72
13. £19

Adding pairs to 100

The bridge can only hold 100 kg safely.

The people cross in pairs.

Write the pairs so that everyone can cross.

60 kg

68 kg

55 kg

26 kg

40 kg

49 kg

32 kg

74 kg

45 kg

51 kg

Explore

Use number cards 0 to 9.

Make pairs of 2-digit numbers.

They must add to make 100.

Write the pairs you find.

0 1 2

6 8 9

5 3 + 4 7

Adding several numbers

Write the cost for each set of books.

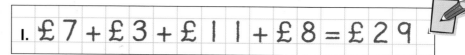

I. £7 + £3 + £11 + £8 = £29

1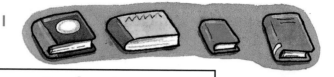

2

Book prices

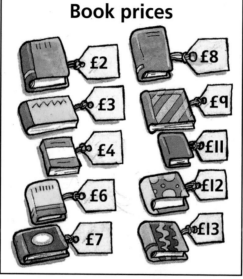

£2 £8
£3 £9
£4 £11
£6 £12
£7 £13

3

4

5

6

7

8

9

10

e Draw 4 sets costing £30.

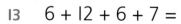

Copy and complete.

II. 4 + 7 + 8 + 9 = 28

11 4 + 7 + 8 + 9 =

13 6 + 12 + 6 + 7 =

15 11 + 8 + 9 + 12 =

17 13 + 11 + 9 + 7 =

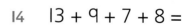

12 8 + 6 + 5 + 4 =

14 13 + 9 + 7 + 8 =

16 4 + 8 + 6 + 2 + 9 =

18 15 + 3 + 5 + 8 + 7 =

Adding several numbers

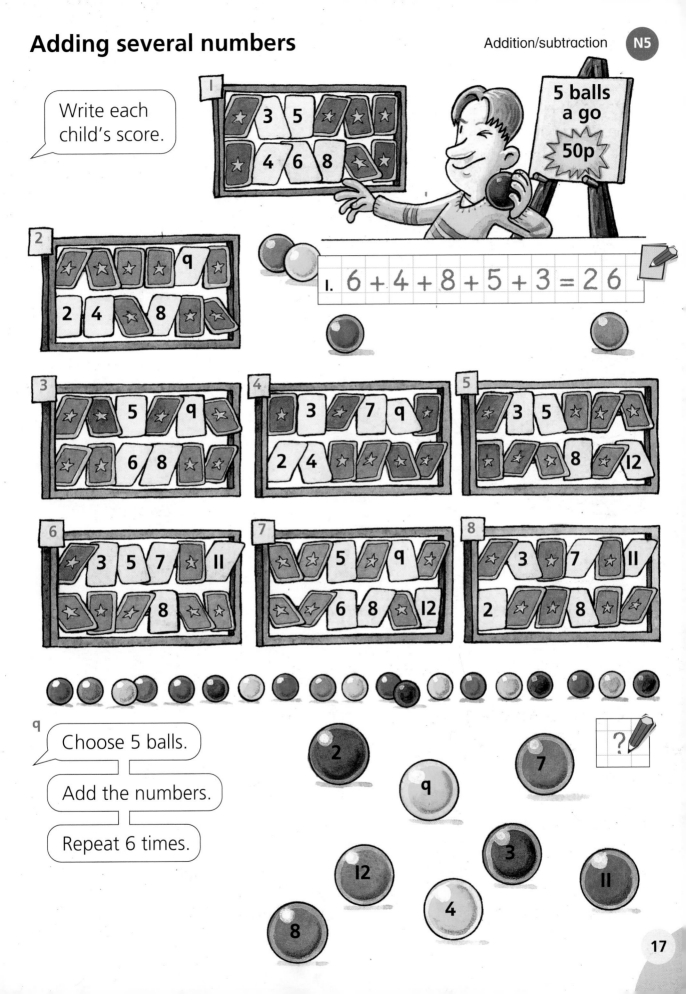

Write each child's score.

5 balls a go

50p

1. $6 + 4 + 8 + 5 + 3 = 26$

Choose 5 balls.

Add the numbers.

Repeat 6 times.

Adding several numbers

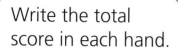

Write the total score in each hand.

1. $5 + 3 + 4 + 9 + 8 = 29$

1. 5 3 4 9 8

2. 10 5 3 8 7

3. 6 9 8 4 9

4. 7 9 11 3 8

5. 9 8 9 2 8

6. 9 6 8 5 8

7. 5 3 14 5 6

8. 4 7 12 9 8

9. 9 11 9 6 6

Explore

Use any of the cards shown.

Find 10 ways to make 19.

2 3 4 5 6 7 8 9

18

Adding several numbers

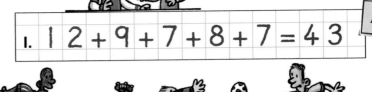

Write the total number of goals scored for each team from September to January.

I. $12 + 9 + 7 + 8 + 7 = 43$

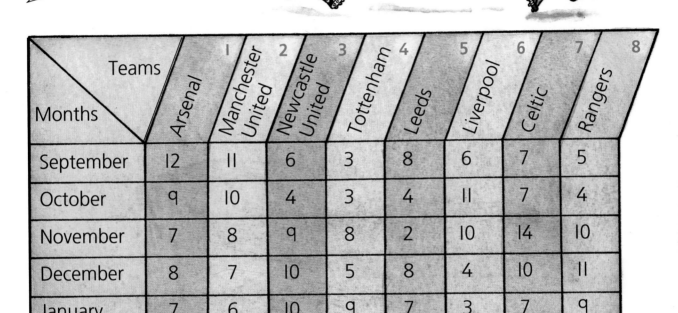

Months \ Teams	1 Arsenal	2 Manchester United	3 Newcastle United	4 Tottenham	5 Leeds	6 Liverpool	7 Celtic	8 Rangers
September	12	11	6	3	8	6	7	5
October	9	10	4	3	4	11	7	4
November	7	8	9	8	2	10	14	10
December	8	7	10	5	8	4	10	11
January	7	6	10	9	7	3	7	9

Each football shirt letter has a value.

Write the cost of your name.

Write the cost of other words.

Value	Letters
6p	d h n p
7p	b m
8p	c g l
9p	f k w y
10p	a e i o u
11p	r s t x
12p	j q v z

e What are the cheapest and the most expensive 5-letter names you can find?

Write the number
1 more and 1 less than
each ticket number.

1. 3 4 7, 3 4 8, 3 4 9

1 Please come to the Ball. 348

2 Please come to the Ball. 229

3 Please come to the Ball. 410

4 Please come to the Ball. 667

5 Please come to the Ball. 399

6 Please come to the Ball. 801

7 Please come to the Ball. 850

8 Please come to the Ball. 310

9 Please come to the Ball. 100

10 Please come to the Ball. 555

11 Please come to the Ball. 738

12 Please come to the Ball. 916

Write the numbers 10 more and 10 less than each ticket number.

Write the next 3 numbers
in the series.

13. 2 0 0, 2 5 0, 3 0 0

13 0 50 100 150

14 100 125 150

15 275 300 325 350

16 175 200 225

17 550 600 650 700

18 900 950 1000

Counting in 25s and 50s

Add 50p to each money box.

Write the new total.

1. £4·50 + 50p = £5·00

I £4·50

2 30p

3 £1·10

4 £2·20

5 £3·40

6 £6·50

7 £2·00

8 £5·20

9 £7·00

10 £4·40

11 £9·30

12 £8·50

13 £7·10

Write the next 3 numbers.

14. 600, 550, 500

14 750 — 700 — 650 —

15 300 — 275 — 250 —

16 900 — 875 — 850 —

17 1000 — 950 — 900 —

18 650 — 600 — 550 —

19 350 — 325 — 300 —

Copy and complete each row of numbers.

I. 7 6 3, 8 1 3, 8 6 3, 9 1 3

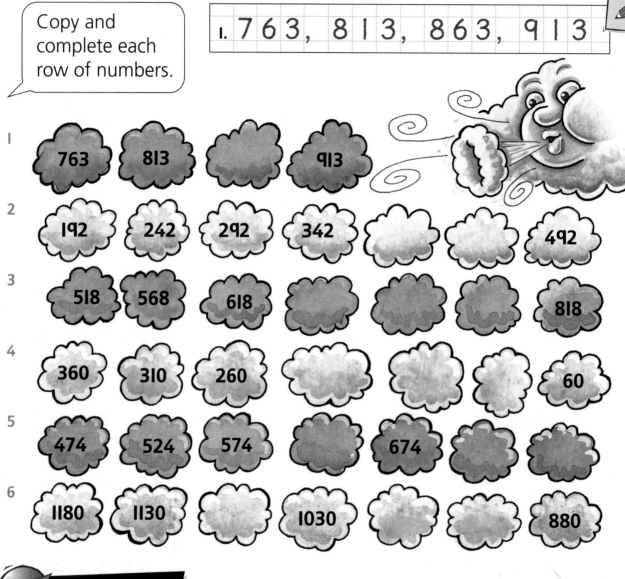

1   763   813   913

2   192   242   292   342   492

3   518   568   618   818

4   360   310   260   60

5   474   524   574   674

6   1180   1130   1030   880

 **Explore**

25   75   50   1000

You are going to write the numbers from 0 to 1000 counting in 25s.

Guess how many numbers ending in 5 you will write then try it.

How many numbers ending in 5 if you wrote the numbers 1000 to 2000 counting in 25s?

Multiplying

Write a multiplication to show how many letters in each set.

1. $2 \times 4 = 8$

2   3   4

Write the pairs of children with the same number of stamps.

1. Neil and Ella
$4 \times 5 = 5 \times 4$

Neil

Kate

Bec

Amos

Mike

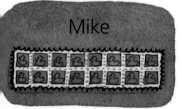

Habeeb

Ella

Jo

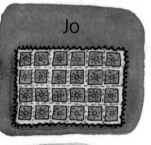

Samira

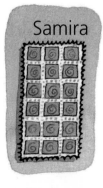

Jane

Bob

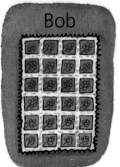

Carlos

Multiplying

Draw a pair of grids to match the number.

I.
$$2 \times 5 = 10$$
$$5 \times 2 = 10$$

1. 10
2. 15
3. 21
4. 8

Draw 2 pairs of grids to match the number.

5. 18
6. 12
7. 24
8. 16

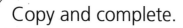

Copy and complete.

Write a matching multiplication.

9. $$8 \times 2 = 16$$
$$2 \times 8 = 16$$

9. $\bigcirc \times 2 = 16$

10. $3 \times \bigcirc = 12$

11. $\bigcirc \times 5 = 10$

12. $6 \times \bigcirc = 18$

13. $\bigcirc \times 10 = 30$

14. $\bigcirc \times 2 = 14$

15. $9 \times \bigcirc = 45$

16. $1 \times \bigcirc = 6$

17. $8 \times \bigcirc = 24$

18. $\bigcirc \times 2 = 18$

19. $5 \times 4 = \bigcirc$

20. $\bigcirc \times 4 = 24$

Multiplying

Screamer 45p   Dipper 55p   Big Wish 60p   Water Splash 35p

Write the total cost for the number of turns.

I 4 turns on Screamer

I. $4 \times 45p = 180p$
$= £1·80$

2 2 turns on Dipper

3 3 turns on Big Wish

4 3 turns on Screamer

5 4 turns on Water Splash

6 5 turns on Screamer

7 3 turns on Dipper

8 5 turns on Big Wish

9 4 turns on Dipper

e Write how many turns on each ride for £5·00.

Explore

How many multiplication pairs can you write with an answer of 24?

How many with an answer of 18? Of 60?

$2 \times 12 = 24$
$3 \times 8 = 24$
$4 \times$

| Each kangaroo can hop a different distance. | Write how far each one travels. |

1. $20 \times 3m = 3m \times 20$
   $= 60m$

1

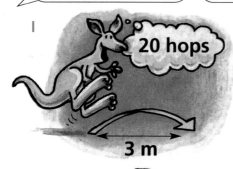

20 hops

3 m

2

30 hops

2 m

3

31 hops

5 m

4

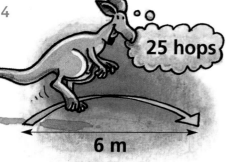

25 hops

6 m

5

38 hops

$\frac{1}{2}$ m

6

35 hops

4 m

ℯ Write how far each kangaroo goes after 40 hops.

7 Jo needs **4** flakes.

They are **60p** each.

She has **£2·00**.

How much more does she need?

8

40p 50p

Mike buys **3** Whizzos and **2** Whackos.

What is the total cost?

Problems

9

Jenny has **3 m** of ribbon.

She cuts **5** lengths, each **40 cm** long.

How much ribbon is left?

10

Raffle tickets cost **30p** each.

Jez buys **5** tickets.

How much change has he from **£2·00**?

Dividing

Write divisions to match.

1

I. $18 \div 3 = 6$

2

3

4

5

6

7

8

9

10

Copy and complete.

11 $20 \div 4 = $

II. $20 \div 4 = 5$

12 $30 \div 3 = $

13 $14 \div 2 = $

Build strips of cubes to help you.

14 $16 \div 4 = $

15 $28 \div 7 = $

16 $18 \div 2 = $

17 $16 \div 2 = $

18 $12 \div 6 = $

19 $20 \div 5 = $

20 $30 \div 10 = $

21 $25 \div 5 = $

22 $24 \div 6 = $

Dividing

Each class lines up in 3 rows.

How many children in each row?

1. $18 \div 3 = 6$
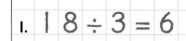

1
Class A
18 children

2
Class B
30 children

3
Class C
15 children

4
Class D
24 children

5
Class E
21 children

6
Class F
33 children

7
Class G
36 children

8
Class H
27 children

9
Class I
39 children

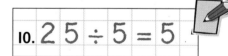
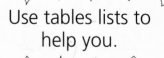

Copy and complete.

10 $25 \div 5 =$

10. $25 \div 5 = 5$

11 $40 \div 5 =$

12 $24 \div$ 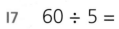 $= 6$

Use tables lists to help you.

13 $28 \div 4 =$

14 $30 \div 10 =$

15 $60 \div$ = 10

16 $14 \div 2 =$

17 $60 \div 5 =$

18 $24 \div 3 =$

19 $36 \div$ $= 9$

20 $27 \div 3 =$

Dosing

Dividing

The apples are packed in rows of 4.

Write how many rows in each box.

I. $20 \div 4 = 5$

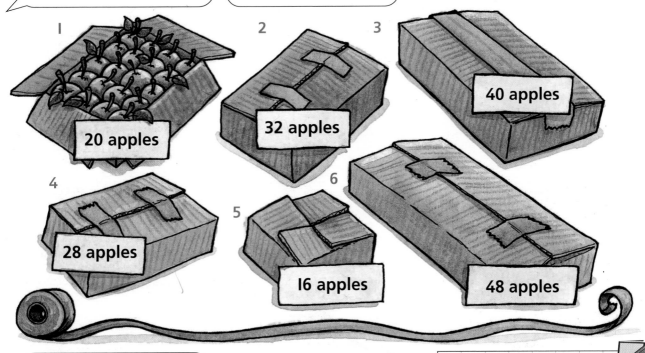

1

20 apples

2

3

40 apples

32 apples

4

6

5

28 apples

16 apples

48 apples

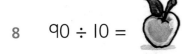

Copy and complete.

7   $40 \div 5 = $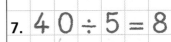

7. $40 \div 5 = 8$

8   $90 \div 10 = $

9   $10 \div \square = 5$

10   $16 \div 4 = $

11   $20 \div 5 = $

12   $21 \div 3 = $

13   $24 \div \square = 4$

14   $30 \div \square = 6$

15   $36 \div 6 = $

16   $24 \div 2 = $

Explore

Find out how many pairs of numbers fit this division.

$$36 \div \square = \square$$

Cut squared paper to help you. Think about different lengths and widths.

29

Dividing

Benji needs strips of wood and tape cut into equal pieces.

Write a division for each.

I. $35\,cm \div 5 = 7\,cm$

1.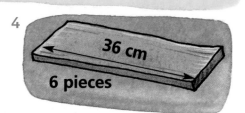
35 cm
5 pieces

2.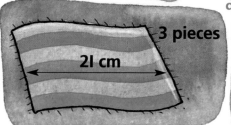
3 pieces
27 cm

3.
44 cm
2 pieces

4.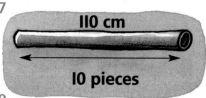
36 cm
6 pieces

5.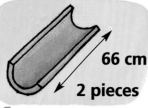
32 cm
4 pieces

6.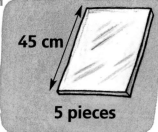
66 cm
2 pieces

7.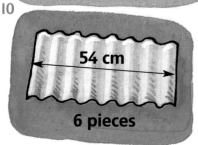
110 cm
10 pieces

8.
3 pieces
21 cm

9.
45 cm
5 pieces

10.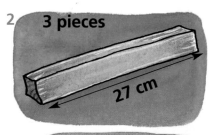
54 cm
6 pieces

@ How many pieces in total?

Problems

11.
24 fish are divided between some cats. Each cat has **4** fish. How many cats?

12.
Each of **3** sisters has **9** biscuits. There are **2** left over. How many biscuits?

13. Sonam had **forty 10p** coins. She grouped them in piles of **5**. How many piles?

14. **4** friends win **£36**. How much each? How much more would they need in total to have **£10** each?

Multiplying

Write the position of the pointer on each counting stick.

la. 6

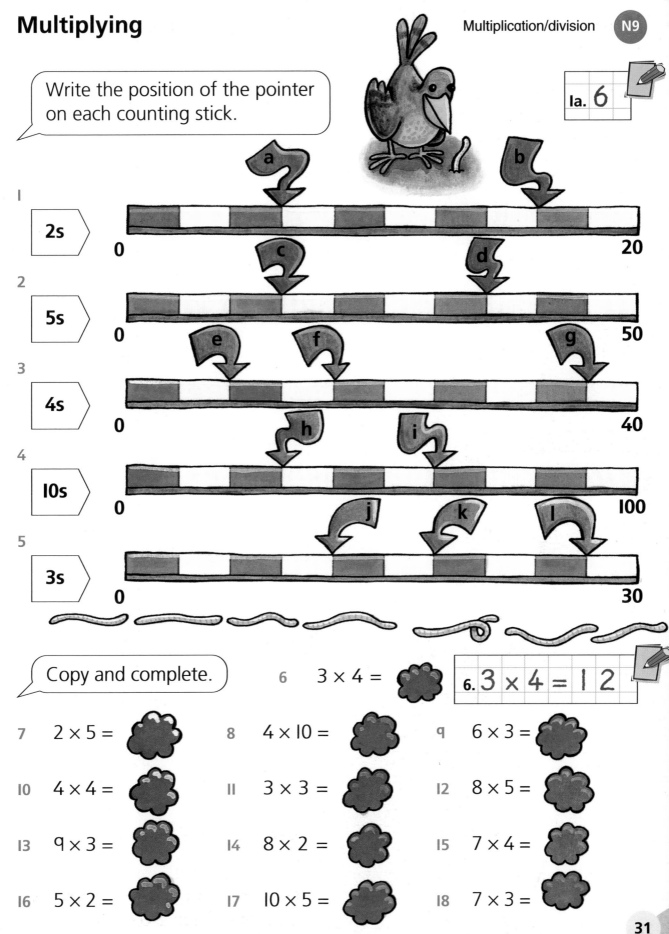

1 **2s**   0 ... 20

2 **5s**   0 ... 50

3 **4s**   0 ... 40

4 **10s** 0 ... 100

5 **3s**   0 ... 30

Copy and complete.

6   $3 \times 4 =$

6. $3 \times 4 = 12$

7   $2 \times 5 =$

8   $4 \times 10 =$

9   $6 \times 3 =$

10 $4 \times 4 =$

11 $3 \times 3 =$

12 $8 \times 5 =$

13 $9 \times 3 =$

14 $8 \times 2 =$

15 $7 \times 4 =$

16 $5 \times 2 =$

17 $10 \times 5 =$

18 $7 \times 3 =$

31

Multiplying and dividing

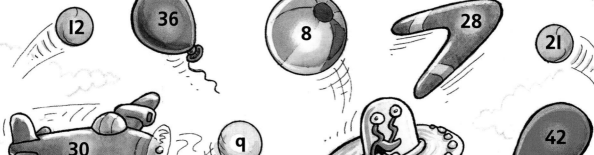

Write the numbers that are:

1 in the ×4 table?

1. 8, 12, …

2 in the ×3 table?

3 in both tables?

4 in neither table?

Copy and complete.

5 8 ÷ 2 =

5. 8 ÷ 2 = 4

6 12 ÷ 3 =

7 5 × 4 =

8 40 ÷ 10 =

9 25 ÷ 5 =

10 7 × 5 =

11 32 ÷ 4 =

12 9 × 3 =

13 18 ÷ 2 =

14 21 ÷ 3 =

Multiplying and dividing

Copy and complete.

1    × 4 = 16

1. $4 \times 4 = 1 \ 6$

2    ÷ 3 = 6

3   5 × 4 =

4   7 ×  = 21

5   ÷ 4 = 5

6   × 3 = 27

7   28 ÷ = 7

8   8 × = 24

9   ÷ 5 = 7

10   × 4 = 12

Explore

Write the grid numbers that are in both tables shown.

1	2	3	4	5	6	7	8	9	10
11	12	13	14	15	16	17	18	19	20
21	22	23	24	25	26	27	28	29	30
31	32	33	34	35	36	37	38	39	40
41	42	43	44	45	46	47	48	49	50
51	52	53	54	55	56	57	58	59	60

11   ×2 and ×3

12   ×3 and ×4

13   ×3 and ×5

14   ×4 and ×5

15   ×3 and ×10

16   ×2 and ×5

17   ×4 and ×10

18   ×2 and ×4

1	2	3	4	5	6	7	8	9	10
11	12	13	14	15	16	17	18	19	20

Colour in squares on a number grid to help you.

e Choose your own pair of tables. Write numbers that appear in both.

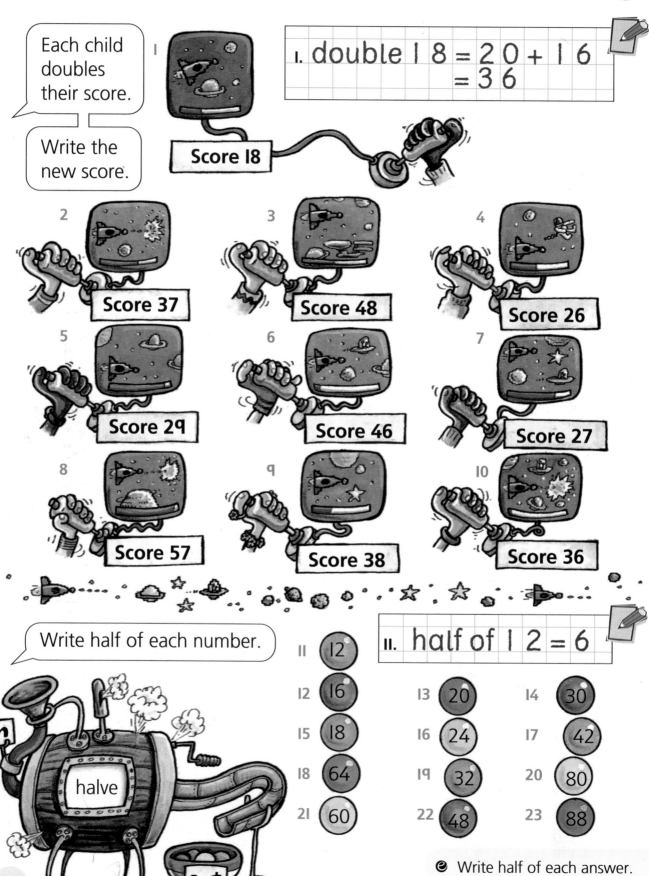

Each child doubles their score.

Write the new score.

I.
Score 18

I. double 18 = 20 + 16
= 36

2 Score 37

3 Score 48

4 Score 26

5 Score 29

6 Score 46

7 Score 27

8 Score 57

9 Score 38

10 Score 36

Write half of each number.

11 12

II. half of 12 = 6

12 16   13 20   14 30

15 18   16 24   17 42

18 64   19 32   20 80

21 60   22 48   23 88

in

halve

out

❷ Write half of each answer.

Doubling

Write the cost of two of each.

1  **23p**

2  **42p**

3 **31p**

4  **18p**

5  **25p**

6 **13p**

7  **35p**

8  **47p**

q  **28p**

10  **22p**

11  **33p**

12  **2qp**

13  **44p**

Copy and complete.

14.

in	20	50	70
out	40	100	140

14

in	20	50		q0	60		80	40
out			140			60		

15

in	15		75	45		85	35
out		110			50		130

35

Doubling and halving

Scores in the red ring count double.

Write the scores.

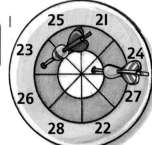

1.
$$\text{double } 23 + 24$$
$$= 46 + 24 = 70$$

2
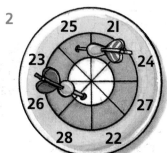

3
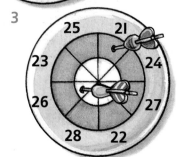

4
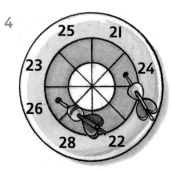

5
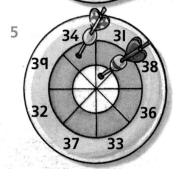

6
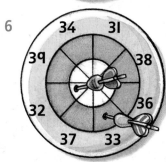

7

8
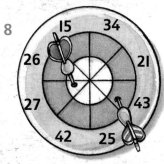

9
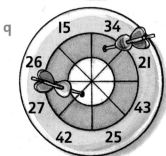

10
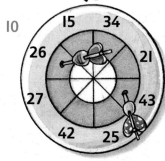

℮ Write the highest score using 2 darts on each board.

Explore

Use the number cards 0 to 9.

Make pairs of **2**-digit numbers BUT… one number must be **half** the other.

How many different pairs can you make?

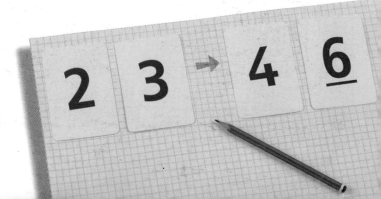

2 3 → 4 6

Fours and eights

> Copy and complete.

1. $2 \times 4 = 8$, $2 \times 8 = 16$

1	$2 \times 4 =$	$2 \times 8 =$
2	$3 \times 4 =$	$3 \times 8 =$
3	$4 \times 4 =$	$4 \times 8 =$
4	$5 \times 4 =$	$5 \times 8 =$
5	$6 \times 4 =$	$6 \times 8 =$
6	$7 \times 4 =$	$7 \times 8 =$

> To find the second answer in each row, double the first answer.

ℓ Double each answer again to get the ×16 table.

> Each creature has 8 legs.

> Write how many legs in each group.

1

1. $3 \times 8 = 24$

2

3

4

5

6

7

8

9

ℓ How many pairs of shoes would each set of creatures need?

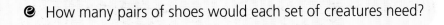

Fours and eights

Write the numbers that are:

1 in the ×4 table

1. 8, 12, …

2 in the ×8 table   3 in both tables   4 in neither table

e Write some more numbers that are in neither table.

Copy and complete.

5 24 ÷ 8 =

5. 24 ÷ 8 = 3

6 40 ÷ 8 =   7 8 ÷ 8 =   8 48 ÷ 8 =

9 16 ÷ 8 =   10 80 ÷ 8 =   11 64 ÷ 8 =

12 32 ÷ 8 =   13 56 ÷ 8 =   14 72 ÷ 8 =

Fours and eights

Double each answer.

Write it in eights (×8).

1. double 4 0 = 8 0
   1 0 × 8 = 8 0

1   $10 \times 4 = 40$

2   $6 \times 4 = 24$

3   $13 \times 4 = 52$

4   $15 \times 4 = 60$

5   $8 \times 4 = 32$

6   $12 \times 4 = 48$

7   $20 \times 4 = 80$

8   $11 \times 4 = 44$

9   $100 \times 4 = 400$

10   $9 \times 4 = 36$

11   $30 \times 4 = 120$

12   $50 \times 4 = 200$

e Write 5 more multiplications like these.

Explore

These numbers are in the ×4 table.

| 4 | 8 | 12 | 16 | 20 | 24 | 28 | 32 | 36 | 40 |

These are their units digits: 4, 8, 2, 6, …

Write more numbers in the ×4 table.

Look for a pattern.

Do the same for numbers in the ×8 table. What do you notice?

Fours and eights

Each badge costs 8p.

Write how much each set costs.

1

I. $3 \times 8p = 24p$

2

3

4

5

6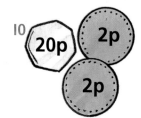

7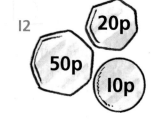

Write the number of badges you could buy.

8

8. $40p \div 8p = 5$

9

10

11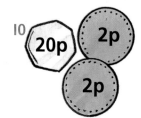

12

---

13 **60** children are put in teams of **8**.

How many teams?

How many children left over?

14 Each rowboat can seat **8** people.

How many people could you get in **7** boats?

Problems

15 Stamps cost **8p**.

Karen has **£1·00**.

How many stamps can she buy?

How much change will she get?

16 The total distance around the octagon is **48 cm**.

Each side is the same length.

How long is each side?

Fractions

Write the fraction of each shape that is blue.

1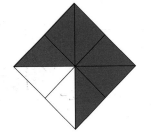

I. $\frac{6}{8}$

2

3

4

5

6

7

8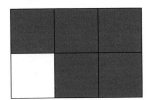

9

10

Write the fractions of each shape that are green and yellow.

11

II. green $\frac{3}{5}$, yellow $\frac{2}{5}$

12

13

14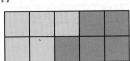

15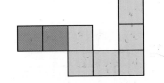

16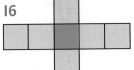

17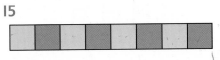

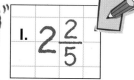

Write how much pizza is left.

1

1. $2\frac{2}{5}$

2

3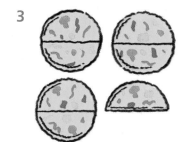

4

5

6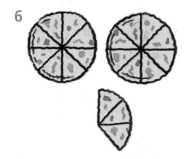

7

℮ What fraction has been eaten, if there were 5 pizzas to start with?

Write the number of blue towers.

8

8. $3\frac{2}{5}$

9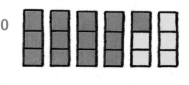

10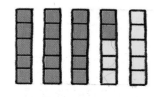

11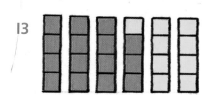

12

13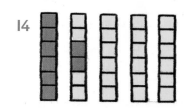

14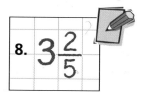

℮ Write the number of yellow towers.

Fractions

Each turn on the computer takes $\frac{1}{4}$ hour.

Write how long each child takes.

I. $1\frac{1}{4}$ hours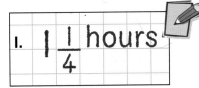

1  5 turns

2  7 turns

3  3 turns

4  8 turns

5  6 turns

6  9 turns

7 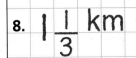 13 turns

The running track is $\frac{1}{3}$ km.

Write the total distance each runner travels.

8. $1\frac{1}{3}$ km

8  4 times round

9  7 times round

10  5 times round

11  10 times round

12  3 times round

13  9 times round

14  12 times round

15 11 times round

16 17 times round

Matching fractions

Write the matching fractions for each pair.

1.

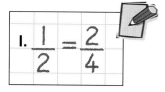
I. $\dfrac{1}{2} = \dfrac{2}{4}$

2.

3.

4.

5.

6.

7.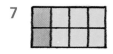

Write the missing numbers to make matching fractions.

8. $\dfrac{2}{4} = \dfrac{1}{2}$

8.
$\dfrac{}{4} = \dfrac{1}{2}$

9.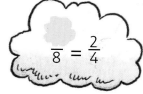
$\dfrac{}{8} = \dfrac{1}{4}$

10.
$\dfrac{}{2} = $ I whole

11.
$\dfrac{}{8} = \dfrac{2}{4}$

I whole	
$\frac{1}{2}$	$\frac{1}{2}$

$\frac{1}{4}$	$\frac{1}{4}$	$\frac{1}{4}$	$\frac{1}{4}$

$\frac{1}{8}$	$\frac{1}{8}$	$\frac{1}{8}$	$\frac{1}{8}$	$\frac{1}{8}$	$\frac{1}{8}$	$\frac{1}{8}$	$\frac{1}{8}$

12.
$\dfrac{}{8} = \dfrac{1}{2}$

13.
$\dfrac{}{4} = $ I whole

14.
$\dfrac{}{8} = \dfrac{3}{4}$

15.
$\dfrac{}{8} = $ I whole

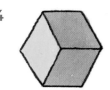
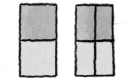

Matching fractions

Copy and colour each grid to match the first fraction.

Write the matching fractions.

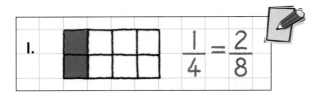

I. $\dfrac{1}{4} = \dfrac{2}{8}$

1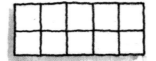

$\dfrac{1}{4} = \dfrac{}{8}$

2

$\dfrac{3}{4} = \dfrac{}{8}$

3

$\dfrac{1}{3} = \dfrac{}{6}$

4

$\dfrac{2}{3} = \dfrac{}{6}$

5

$\dfrac{1}{5} = \dfrac{}{10}$

6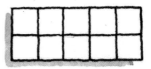

$\dfrac{4}{5} = \dfrac{}{10}$

e On squared paper draw some more matching fractions.

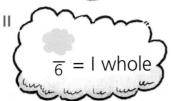

Write the missing numbers to make matching fractions.

7

$\dfrac{}{6} = \dfrac{1}{3}$

8

$\dfrac{}{6} = \dfrac{2}{3}$

q

$\dfrac{}{6} = \dfrac{1}{2}$

10

$\dfrac{}{3} = 1 \text{ whole}$

11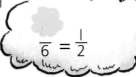

$\dfrac{}{6} = 1 \text{ whole}$

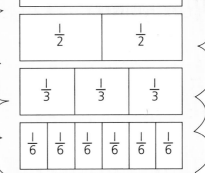

1 whole	
$\frac{1}{2}$	$\frac{1}{2}$

$\frac{1}{3}$	$\frac{1}{3}$	$\frac{1}{3}$

$\frac{1}{6}$	$\frac{1}{6}$	$\frac{1}{6}$	$\frac{1}{6}$	$\frac{1}{6}$	$\frac{1}{6}$

Matching fractions

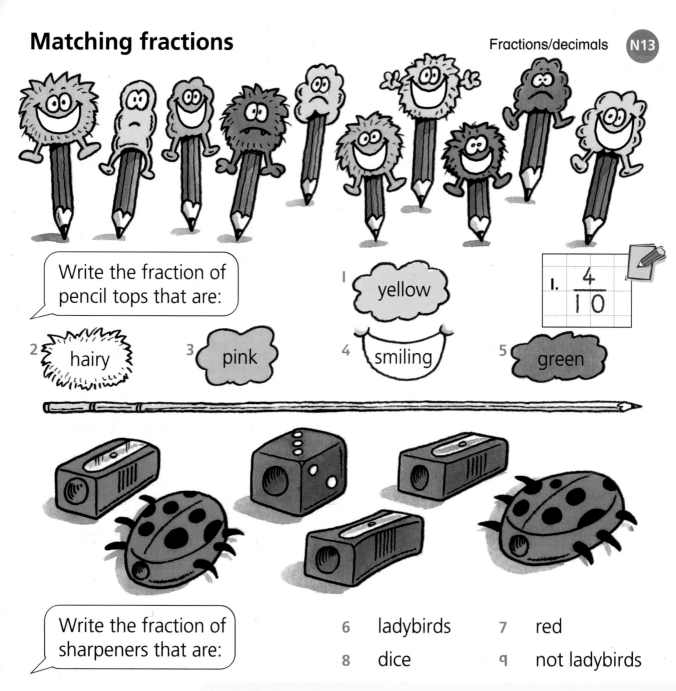

Write the fraction of pencil tops that are:

1 yellow

I. $\dfrac{4}{10}$

2 hairy

3 pink

4 smiling

5 green

Write the fraction of sharpeners that are:

6 ladybirds

7 red

8 dice

9 not ladybirds

e Write matching fractions for any of these fractions that you can.

Explore

Use the number cards I to I0.

Choose 4 to make a pair of matching fractions like this:

$$\dfrac{1}{3} = \dfrac{2}{6}$$

How many different pairs can you make?

Complete the additions.

Use the grid and the spiders to help you.

ı. $4 + 30 = 34$

1   $4 + 30 = $

2   $17 + 19 = $

3   $23 + 29 = $

4   $38 + 29 = $

5   $45 + 29 = $

6   $52 + 39 = $

7   $66 + 19 = $

8   $79 + 21 = $

9   $81 + 11 = $

10   $94 + 39 = $

1	2	3		5	6	7	8	9	10
11	12	13	14	15	16		18	19	20
21	22		24	25	26	27	28	29	30
31	32	33	34	35	36	37		39	40
41	42	43	44		46	47	48	49	50
51		53	54	55	56	57	58	59	60
61	62	63	64	65		67	68	69	70
71	72	73	74	75	76	77	78		80
	82	83	84	85	86	87	88	89	90
91	92	93		95	96	97	98	99	100

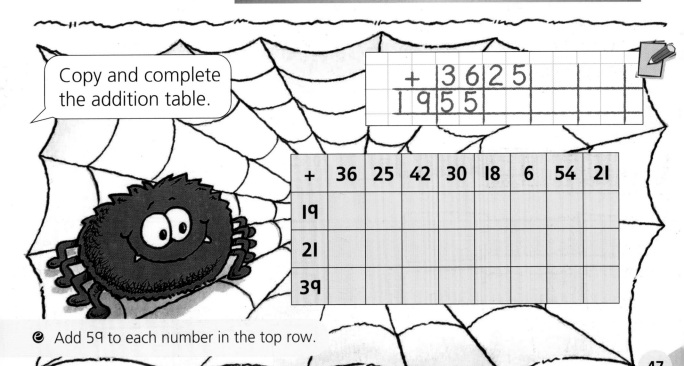

Copy and complete the addition table.

$$+\ 3\ 6\ 2\ 5$$
$$1\ 9\ 5\ 5$$

+	36	25	42	30	18	6	54	21
19								
21								
39								

ℓ Add 59 to each number in the top row.

Add 32 to each <u>red</u> number.

I. $14 + 32 = 46$

1	2	3	4	5	6	7	8	9	10
11	12	13	<u>14</u>	15	16	17	18	19	20
21	22	23	24	25	26	<u>27</u>	28	29	30
31	32	33	34	35	36	37	<u>38</u>	39	40
41	42	43	44	(45)	<u>46</u>	47	(48)	49	50
(51)	52	53	<u>54</u>	55	56	(57)	58	59	60
61	62	63	(64)	65	66	<u>67</u>	68	(69)	70
71	72	(73)	74	<u>75</u>	76	77	78	79	80
<u>81</u>	82	83	84	85	(86)	87	88	89	90
91	(92)	<u>93</u>	94	(95)	96	97	<u>98</u>	99	100

Subtract 29 from each (blue) number.

II. $45 - 29 = 16$

Copy and complete.

 20 $275 - 29 = $ ✿

20. $275 - 29 = 246$

 21 $432 - 29 = $ ✿

22 $556 + 39 = $ ✿

23 $674 - 39 = $ ✿

24 $783 - 49 = $ ✿

25 $326 + 49 = $ ✿

26 $245 - 39 = $ ✿

Adding near multiples of 10

The price of all spring toys is going up by 39p.

Write the new prices.

I. 45p + 39p = 84p

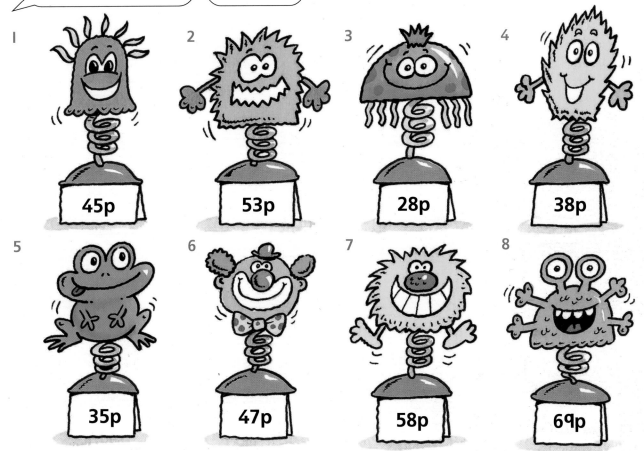

1. 45p

2. 53p

3. 28p

4. 38p

5. 35p

6. 47p

7. 58p

8. 69p

ℓ Each price goes down 11p instead. Write the new prices.

Explore

Four numbers add to make this number.

All four numbers end in 9.

The first digits are all different.

Find what the four numbers could be.

Start by trying any four numbers, for example 69, 79, 39, 19.

236

Subtracting near multiples of 10

The computer subtracts 29 points from everyone's score!

Write the new scores.

1. Score 132

1. $132 - 29 = 103$

2. Score 246

3. Score 381

4. Score 163

5. Score 154

6. Score 443

7. Score 262

8. Score 191

9. Score 285

Problems

10. Dilek has **67p**. She buys a lolly for **39p**. Dad gives her **50p**. How much money has she now?

11. Tom watches an **82 minute** video. He then watches the News for **19 minutes**. He then watches a comedy for **29 minutes**. For how long did he watch TV?

12. Jon has saved **£42**. He spends **£19**. Then his uncle gives him **£32**. How much has he now?

Adding multiples of 10

Copy and complete each pair of additions.

1 24 + 13
240 + 130

```
1. 2 4 + 1 3 = 3 7
   2 4 0 + 1 3 0 = 3 7 0
```

2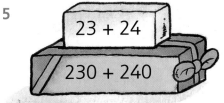
16 + 12
160 + 120

3
17 + 5
170 + 50

4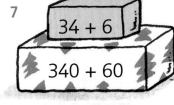
25 + 8
250 + 80

5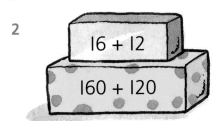
23 + 24
230 + 240

6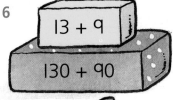
13 + 9
130 + 90

7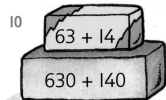
34 + 6
340 + 60

8
15 + 7
150 + 70

9
42 + 21
420 + 210

10
63 + 14
630 + 140

e Write five addition pairs like these of your own.

Each paper chain has 140 cm added to it.

Write the new length.

```
II. 2 3 0 + 1 4 0 = 3 7 0 cm
```

11
230 cm

12
310 cm

13
210 cm

14
420 cm

15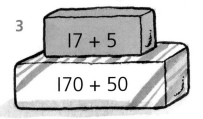
360 cm

16
750 cm

17
860 cm

Adding multiples of 10

Complete each set of additions.

1
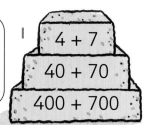
4 + 7
40 + 70
400 + 700

1. 4 + 7 = 11
40 + 70 = 110
400 + 700 = 1100

2
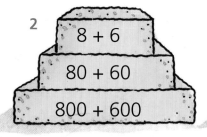
8 + 6
80 + 60
800 + 600

3
16 + 7 (3 + 12)
3 + 12
30 + 120
300 + 1200

4
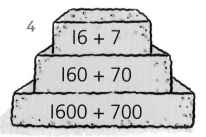
16 + 7
160 + 70
1600 + 700

5
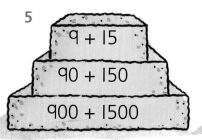
9 + 15
90 + 150
900 + 1500

6
13 + 9
130 + 90
1300 + 900

7
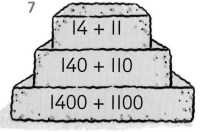
14 + 11
140 + 110
1400 + 1100

8
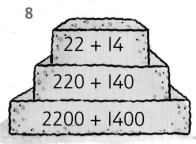
22 + 14
220 + 140
2200 + 1400

9
7 + 17
70 + 170
700 + 1700

10
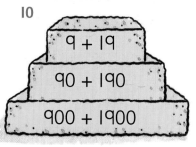
9 + 19
90 + 190
900 + 1900

Add £50 to each safe.

?

11 £140

12 £230

13 £310

14 £440

Each new amount is made up to £500. Write the amount needed for each safe.

Subtracting multiples of 10

Copy and complete.

1 13 – 7
130 – 70

1. $13 - 7 = 6$
$130 - 70 = 60$

2 18 – 9
180 – 90

3 24 – 8
240 – 80

4 21 – 6
210 – 60

5 34 – 7
340 – 70

6 23 – 12
230 – 120

7 36 – 8
360 – 80

8 42 – 9
420 – 90

9 27 – 13
270 – 130

10 63 – 9
630 – 90

11 540 – 110

12 170 – 80

13 210 – 110

700 cm are chopped off each log to make wardrobes.

Write how much is left.

14. $1200 - 700$
$= 500 \, cm$

14 ← 1200 cm →

15 ← 1500 cm →

16 ← 2100 cm →

17 ← 2400 cm →

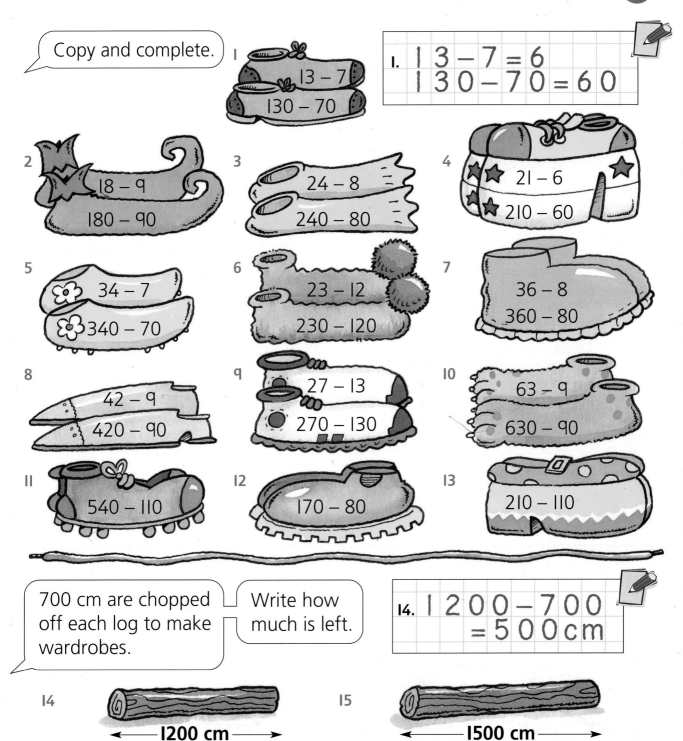

e Another 400 cm are used to make matching tables. How much is left now?

53

Copy and complete the subtractions.

1.
23 – 12
230 – 120
2300 – 1200

I. 23 – 12 = 11
230 – 120 = 110
2300 – 1200 = 1100

2
32 – 6
320 – 60
3200 – 600

3
28 – 7
280 – 70
2800 – 700

4
21 – 9
210 – 90
2100 – 900

5
17 – 11
170 – 110
1700 – 1100

6
16 – 8
160 – 80
1600 – 800

7
34 – 12
340 – 120
3400 – 1200

8
45 – 9
450 – 90
4500 – 900

9
53 – 11
530 – 110
5300 – 1100

10
49 – 13
490 – 130
4900 – 1300

e Add the answers to the bottom steps on the last 6 questions.

Problems

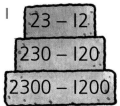

11 Sandy is on page **80** in her reading book.

She reads **30** more pages.

The next day she reads another **20** pages.

What page is she on now?

12 There is **£270** in the safe.

The banker adds **£80** at the end of the day.

The next day **£150** is taken out.

How much is left?

4-digit numbers

Write the next three numbers.

1. 2 3 1 7, 2 3 1 8, 2 3 1 9

	1	2	3
Counting in 1s	2316	4239	3107
	4	5	6
Counting in 10s	5436	4720	3190
	7	8	9
Counting in 100s	4316	7904	2079
	10	11	12
Counting in 1000s	3825	4167	3006

e Write the three numbers before.

The coach numbers are in order. Write the missing number.

13. 2 3 4 9

13

2350 2351

14
3428 3427

15
2475 2473

16
2649 2651

17
3088 3089

18
4101 4100

19
2798 2800

20
3118 3117

4-digit numbers

Write the missing numbers.

I.
	22	
31	32	
	42	

I. 3 3

2.
	▢	
122	123	124
	133	

3.
	335	
▢	345	346
	355	

4.
	▢	
587	588	
	598	

5.
	51	
141	151	161
	▢	

6.
	282	
372	382	
	482	

7.
407	417	427
	517	

8.
	446	
▢	546	556
	▢	

9.
	▢	
750	760	
	860	

10.
	330	
420	▢	
	530	

Write each date 10 years later.

II. 1964

II. 1 9 7 4

12. 1492

13. 571

14. 1066

15. 1808

16. 1590

17. 1666

18. 1329

19. 1999

e Write the new dates in order from earliest to latest.

3-digit and 4-digit numbers

Each car drives another 100 km.

Write how far they have driven.

1. 2 2 5 6 k m

1

2 1 5 6 km

2

4 6 8 2 km

3

3 3 4 5 km

4

7 1 3 4 km

5

5 8 0 4 km

6

6 0 4 9 km

7

2 8 7 3 km

8

9 3 2 0 km

9

9 2 3 0 km

10

4 9 5 1 km

11

4 3 1 0 km

12

1 0 4 3 km

Write the distances in order from smallest to largest.

1 1 4 3 km, 2 2 5 6 km, ...

Explore

Use the number cards shown.

Make a pair of 4-digit numbers with a difference of:

| 2 | 2 | 4 | 4 | 8 | 8 |

| 7 | 7 | 3 | 5 | 9 |

1   10   100   1000

Adding several 2-digit numbers

Find two numbers the same colour.

Add the two numbers.

Add 25.

Write the total.

Repeat for each pair.

1. $26 + 37 + 25 = 88$

1	2	3	4	5	6	7	8	9	10
11	12	13	14	15	16	17	18	19	20
21	22	23	24	25	26	27	28	29	30
31	32	33	34	35	36	37	38	39	40
41	42	43	44	45	46	47	48	49	50
51	52	53	54	55	56	57	58	59	60
61	62	63	64	65	66	67	68	69	70
71	72	73	74	75	76	77	78	79	80
81	82	83	84	85	86	87	88	89	90
91	92	93	94	95	96	97	98	99	100

Copy and complete.

8. $35 + 43 + 25 = 103$

8   $35 + 43 + 25$

9   $62 + 17 + 25$

10   $42 + 25 + 37$

11   $51 + 19 + 26$

12   $38 + 42 + 16$

13   $24 + 32 + 28$

14   $35 + 28 + 17$

15   $43 + 22 + 18$

Write how much each child spends.

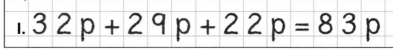

1. 3 2 p + 2 9 p + 2 2 p = 8 3 p

1

29p 32p 22p

2

27p 34p 17p

3

38p 36p 25p

4

36p 22p 17p

5

34p 36p 22p

6

29p 27p 38p

7

32p 38p 17p

● Choose 3 items for each of 3 friends. Write the total cost.

Copy and complete.

8 35 + 45 + 17

9 96 + 4 + 18

10 42 + 37 + 19

11 52 + 25 + 18

12 43 + 34 + 25

13 27 + 28 + 29

14 48 + 45 + 35

15 28 + 38 + 48

Adding several 2-digit numbers

> Write the 3 numbers to add to make each total.

1 **105**

2 **108**

3 **106**

4 **91**

5 **107**

6 **100**

7 **121**

8 **92**

9 **115**

10 **98**

℮ There are four totals not written here. Find out what they are.

Problems

11 Fred is up to page **72** in his reading book.

He reads **32** pages on Monday.

He reads **47** pages on Tuesday.

Which page does he start reading on Wednesday?

12 Safa has saved **£48** for her holiday.

Her uncle gives her **£22** more.

Her gran gives her **£27**.

How much does she have to take away with her?

> Each cyclist visits 4 towns.

> Write the total number of km they cycle.

1. $27 + 15 + 13 = 55$ km

I   Orion to Sirius to Rigel to Spico

2   Antares to Spico to Mira to Sirius

3   Altair to Mira to Sirius to Rigel

4   Spico to Antares to Altair to Mira

5   Antares to Spico to Rigel to Orion

6   Altair to Spico to Rigel to Sirius

7   Orion to Antares to Spico to Altair

8   Rigel to Spico to Altair to Antares

Map:

Orion — 27 km — Sirius

Orion — 12 km — Rigel

Orion — 12 km — Antares

Rigel — 15 km — Sirius

Rigel — 13 km — Spico

Sirius — 26 km — Spico

Antares — 24 km — Rigel

Antares — 9 km — Altair

Antares — 22 km — Spico

Spico — 8 km — Mira

Altair — 23 km — Mira

Explore

$$ab + ac + cd = ea$$

Each letter stands for a different digit.

Work out which digit stands for which letter.

Adding multiples of 10

Copy and complete the additions.

1. | 3 | 4 | 2 |

    | 4 | 0 |

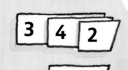

1. $342 + 40 = 382$

2. | 7 | 2 | 5 |

    | 3 | 0 |

3. | 5 | 5 | 1 |

    | 4 | 0 |

4. | 3 | 2 | 9 |

    | 5 | 0 |

5. | 2 | 1 | 8 |

    | 7 | 0 |

6. | 4 | 2 | 4 |

    | 7 | 0 |

7. | 6 | 4 | 3 |

    | 4 | 0 |

8. | 1 | 8 | 3 |

    | 1 | 0 |

9. | 3 | 2 | 5 |

    | 7 | 0 |

10. | 4 | 6 | 9 |

    | 3 | 0 |

These people get a £50 bonus in their pay.

Write how much they get in total.

II. $£445 + £50 = £495$

11 £445

12 £225

13 £342

14 £236

15 £320

16 £516

Adding multiples of 10

Each runner sprints the last part of the race.

Write the total length of each race.

I. $216 + 80 = 296$ m

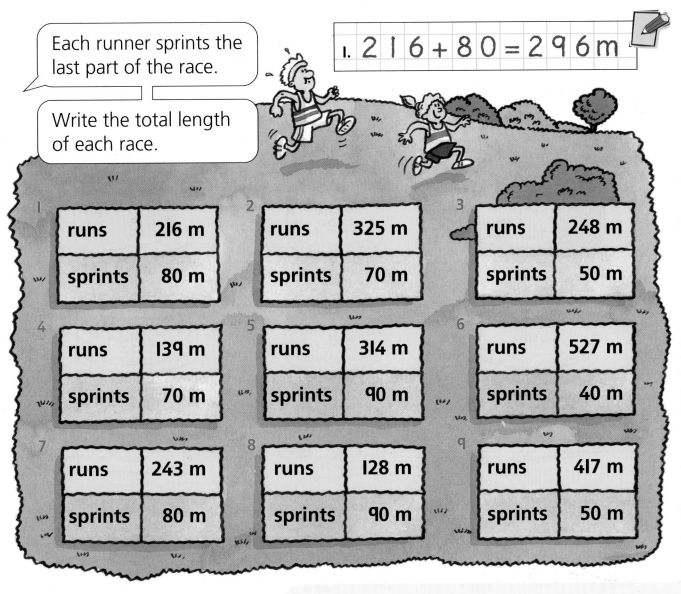

1.

runs	216 m
sprints	80 m

2.

runs	325 m
sprints	70 m

3.

runs	248 m
sprints	50 m

4.

runs	139 m
sprints	70 m

5.

runs	314 m
sprints	90 m

6.

runs	527 m
sprints	40 m

7.

runs	243 m
sprints	80 m

8.

runs	128 m
sprints	90 m

9.

runs	417 m
sprints	50 m

✐ Each runs another 200 m. Write the total distance.

Explore

Use the cards shown.

Find as many additions as you can to make 505.

10 30 20 40 60 80 50 70 90 400 5

465 + 40 = 505

Adding multiples of 10 and 100

Each family saves another £160 towards their holiday.

Write their new total.

1. £117 + £160 = £277

 1 Scotland £117

2  HOL'S £239

3  Florida £406

4  Spain £319

5  Ireland £224

6  Cornwall £133

7  Majorca £253

8  Lake District £111

q £142

Problems

10 Charlie's cricket team has scored **358** runs. | Charlie scores another **20** runs. | Mani scores **30**. | What is the final score?

11 Gemma's team has scored **421** runs. | Melita scores **40** more runs. | Kim scores **20** runs. | What is the final score?

12 Grandad's team has scored **451** runs. | Grandma scores **30** runs. | Uncle Ben scores **10**. | What is the final score?

Copy and complete.

I. $43 - 27 = 16$

Use the number line.

0

100

| 1 | 43 – 27 |
| 2 | 42 – 18 |

| 3 | 72 – 38 |
| 4 | 61 – 25 |

10

| 5 | 54 – 17 |
| 6 | 64 – 27 |

90

| 7 | 44 – 26 |
| 8 | 56 – 38 |

| 9 | 62 – 25 |
| 10 | 73 – 28 |

20

80

| 11 | 51 – 25 |
| 12 | 82 – 38 |

| 13 | 84 – 36 |
| 14 | 75 – 17 |

70

| 15 | 43 – 25 |
| 16 | 53 – 24 |

30

| 17 | 64 – 28 |
| 18 | 74 – 38 |

40

50

60

Subtracting 2-digit numbers

> Everyone has to read as far as page 82 for homework.

> Write how many pages each child still has to read?

I. $82 - 53 = 29$

1 — 53
2 — 66
3 — 35
4 — 58
5 — 48
6 — 37
7 — 45
8 — 27
9 — 64
10 — 55
11 — 25
12 — 63

Explore

There are two numbers. They have a difference of 25.

The digits of one number add to make 8.

What are the two numbers?

Find as many answers as you can.

> Think about 2-digit numbers.

Subtracting 2-digit numbers

> Write the difference in time between the pairs of videos.

I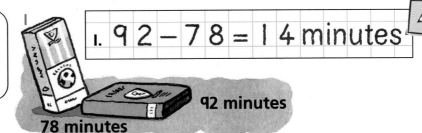

I. $92 - 78 = 14$ minutes

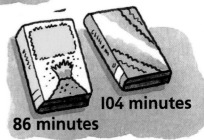

92 minutes

78 minutes

2

58 minutes

84 minutes

3

92 minutes

38 minutes

4

104 minutes

86 minutes

5

62 minutes

94 minutes

6

92 minutes

112 minutes

7

86 minutes

67 minutes

8

91 minutes

125 minutes

9

64 minutes

110 minutes

10

66 minutes

98 minutes

ℓ Write the total time for each pair of videos.

> Copy and complete.

II $83 - 47$

I2 $61 - 28$

I3 $52 - 18$

I4 $72 - 37$

I5 $92 - 45$

I6 $64 - 26$

I7 $55 - 18$

I8 $73 - 25$

I9 $87 - 36$

20 $94 - 27$

Subtracting 2-digit numbers

Copy and complete.

1. 63 – 35

2. 72 – 25
3. 81 – 43
4. 93 – 38

5. 65 – 28
6. 73 – 37
7. 82 – 45

8. 54 – 28
9. 64 – 17
10. 51 – 23

Copy and complete.

11. 63 – 8

12. 72 – 7
13. 54 – 8
14. 41 – 7

15. 33 – 8
16. 62 – 7
17. 91 – 8

18. 42 – 5
19. 34 – 8
20. 63 – 7

Copy and complete.

21. 72 – 29

22. 54 – 19
23. 61 – 39
24. 75 – 49

25. 37 – 19
26. 64 – 49
27. 71 – 29

28. 66 – 29
29. 55 – 39
30. 46 – 19

Subtracting 2-digit numbers

Write the difference in swimming times.

I
53 seconds
35 seconds

I. $53 - 35 = 18$ seconds

2
62 seconds
25 seconds

3
36 seconds
81 seconds

4
39 seconds
74 seconds

5
64 seconds
37 seconds

6
44 seconds   **19 seconds**

7
29 seconds
34 seconds

℮ Write the total time for each pair.

To pass the music test you need 45 points.

How much more has each child scored?

8. $72 - 45 = 27$

8    **72 points**

9 **68 points**

10  **92 points**

11  **73 points**

12 **62 points**

13 **58 points**

Write how much each snake has grown over the year.

I

$$1. \ 9 \ 1 - 6 \ 8 = 2 \ 3 \ cm$$

Jan	Dec
68 cm	91 cm

2

Jan	Dec
29 cm	45 cm

3

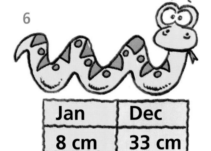

Jan	Dec
64 cm	93 cm

4

Jan	Dec
18 cm	42 cm

5

Jan	Dec
29 cm	51 cm

6

Jan	Dec
8 cm	33 cm

7

Jan	Dec
75 cm	88 cm

Problems

8 Molly cycles **62 km** to the beach.

On the way back she stops after **37 km**.

How much further to go?

9 Sanjay sets his video, but the clock is slow. The video starts **42 minutes** late.

BUT...the programme started **15 minutes** late.

How much did he miss?

10 Peter needs **125 g** of nuts for his cake.

He has **82 g**. How many more does he need?

Subtracting 2-digit numbers

Each cyclist has a 2-day ride.

Write the difference in km between day 1 and day 2.

1.

$$1. \quad 74 - 58 = 16 \text{ km}$$

1.

Day 1	Day 2
74 km	58 km

2

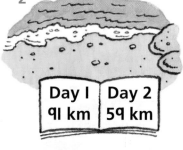

Day 1	Day 2
91 km	59 km

3

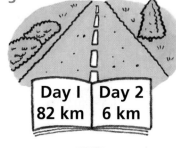

Day 1	Day 2
82 km	6 km

4

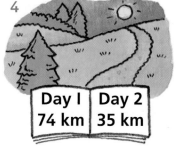

Day 1	Day 2
74 km	35 km

5

Day 1	Day 2
66 km	29 km

6

Day 1	Day 2
72 km	8 km

7

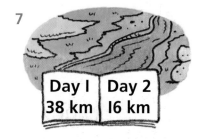

Day 1	Day 2
38 km	16 km

8

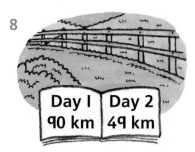

Day 1	Day 2
90 km	49 km

9

Day 1	Day 2
75 km	39 km

10

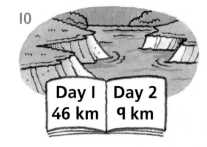

Day 1	Day 2
46 km	9 km

e How far does each cyclist ride in 2 days?

 **Explore**

Gareth and Dave have pocket money each week.

The total amount is less than £1.

Dave has 45p less than Gareth.

Find the different amounts they could get.

Mixed problems

1

Think of a number

Add 5

Double it

Cross off the last digit

Repeat 5 times

Subtract 8

Halve it

Subtract 20

Multiply by 10

What do you notice?
Why do you think it happens?

2

Jen has **£6**.
Tom has **£19**.
They put it all together.

They go shopping and spend **£5**.

Jen's mum gives her a **£10** note.

Tom and Jen go to the cinema. The tickets are **£4** each.

CINEMA £4

They share all the money left over.

How much do they each have?

3

Find the Mystery Number.

It has 2 digits.

If you add 29 you get a number in the ×9 table.

If you halve it you get a number between 15 and 20.

If you subtract 19 you get a number in the ×5 table.

Its digits are consecutive.